Me, Myself and I

Tuscany 2016

Me, Myself and I

Sondra Schwartz

REGENT PRESS
Berkeley, California

Back Cover: SF Bay from Sausalito on a full moon night

: Copyright © 2019 Sondra Schwartz
ISBN 13: 978-1-58790-504-9
ISBN 10: 1-58790-504-3
Liabrary of Congress Catalog Number: 2019937103

Manufactured in the U.S.A.
REGENT PRESS
www.regentpress.net

1972 *UC Berkeley Campus* *Age 28*

I am a student forever and a teacher always.
My people will know that my words are to be valued,
because my words are authentically my own.
Speak to me not of lesser things.
I value the words which come from your mind and heart and mouth,
As I value my own hard earned knowledge.

BEING REBORN

When it's time to be reborn,
Since no one asks you if you wish to be born in the first place,
Why should it come as a surprise,
When no one asks you,
When it is time, if you wish to be reborn?

Each Spring of your life, you are reborn.
It is easy compared to the dying times!
It is hopeful and peaceful and easy!

At rebirth, as at birth, there is no need to ask why.
Because by the time you can speak about it,
It is too late for whys. So when it is time to be reborn,
Enjoy each rebirth as soon a you realize that your new Spring is here.

I guess that is what makes those of us who are wise as wise as we are.
As we begin to die each Winter,
We must remind ourselves that Spring will follow close behind.
We are wise enough to know that following death is a rebirth;
following Winter is Spring.
That the beginning comes after the end!

Instead of the way they told us about it in the story books, when we were kids:
"And they lived happily ever after." Are you kidding? That was NOT the end of the story.
It was not even winter yet. I'm speaking of The Winter of Our Discontent.

The stories should end: And they kept on dying. And they kept on being reborn.

Is he waiting like I did?

One of my students at a Berkeley civil rights demonstration

Waiting until he gets out of high school for life to start?

For learning is discovering a method for living every moment

And for being aware of the choice to live that moment well.

Learning is discovering

that once you realize your choices

are your way of determining your own destiny,

you can accept responsibility for yourself

and create your life the way you want it to be.

You must know what you want; one focus at a time.

Do not get distracted until you achieve that goal.

YES!

You must be clear about choosing one goal; then work to complete it.

Learning requires

a consciousness,

an awareness of the pathway of forward action

which we must maintain.

1979
Age 34

Learning requires

a readiness to listen,

to hear and to understand;

A readiness to look beyond the surface

and into meaning.

2011 *Frog Hollow Farm* *Age 67*

Learning requires

being able to be with yourself,

To feel your own value,

and your own importance

and to allow your feelings to exist.

1948 The Ohio State University
Daddy's Master's Degree graduation
(Me at three, holding my doll Janie.)

1973   One of my ESL students at Holy Names College

Learning requires

being able to look

and to see without judgement,

To be ready to see and to be seen,

To feel seen and to feel heard.

Most honored of all

are those relationships in which

in which teaching and learning are reciprocal.

I always learn from my students;

frequently find myself teaching my teachers.

We must accept our own ability to learn;

to pursue knowledge of our true interests

as soon as we discover them.

Learning requires

making conscious choices

of exactly whom our teachers

and advisors must be.

1983 *Portrait taken for Oakland Teacher's Exhibit* *Age 39*

1986   *Dancespace Studio*   Age 42

learning requires

practicing these important bits

of knowledge over and over again

I am a poet and a cook.
I am a sculptor and a tailor.
I am a Buddhist and a sailor.
I am a recovering codependent and an addict in recovery.
I am a Qi Gong Practitioner and a meditator.

I practice discernment and equanimity. I release my inner critic.
I have an open heart. I live in harmony. I walk in balance.
I am a student forever and a teacher always.

1989   *Self Portrait*   *Age 45*

1067 STARLINGS

One thousand sixty seven starlings flew over me at dawn.
Extraordinary sunrise.
Starlings patterning lace.
A silent voice spoke to each bird: Wings all at once turned right!

Moments pass; then an unseen hand:
A single hundred wings turned
by strategic air command
Lifted and pulled apart from the flock.
Intuition? Updraft? Breeze? Common mind thought?
On high someone decides and as I watch a miracle:
The sky divides!

It was a Van Gogh cornfield on that November morn,
A rush of color: gold and bronze,
A painted canvas not yet formed.
1067 birds made morning look like night
above rows and rows of grapevines, a second pattern hill delight
from which 1067 starlings rose up and took flight !

I never saw those birds before, which I looked up again to see,
Such tiny black laced wings of perfect symmetry !
It was as if a choreographer wrote a design in time :
"Take off is at seven! Meet here to make the rhyme."
Little spaceships fly in unison, in tow.
At first they moved as one, together.
Then at once, apart they flow.

In several fine directions, their flight commanders said,

First one wing, then two hundred others

Moving all, so singly together, I was sure that they were lovers!

One second, then a hundred more move off in a new direction.

Three hundred wings turn, still again, five flights in vivisection!

They separate and then unite in patterns, with no sound

How could so many birds participate unbound?

How could they all be born in one small field, I'll never know.

One thousand eggs in one hundred nests create a faceless sky!

1067 birds; 3124 wings fly by!

Much earlier today, I saw three birds turn and lift and fly!

Then twenty two uplifted and returned up to their sky!

I drove beneath them, as their wings all caught the sun.

N'er will I 'er see this sight again!

My sight must not go unsung!

To simplify a thought into a single line of poetry becomes complex.

To assure a loved one that she is loved becomes almost impossible.

To be aware of the space between thoughts

brings peace and stillness to a cluttered mind.

LET ME LOVE MYSELF !

Let all of you learn to love yourselves.

Only then will we be capable of loving one another.

Only then will we be capable of assuring one another of that love.

1978 Self Portrait. (I finally looked like 17 magazine when I was 35.)

I SPEAK FOR THE YOUNG

I speak

for the young

for we have needs.

We need no more than anyone else,

But we do not know yet who we are

So our needs are more desperate.

I speak for the young

1979 *Age 36*

because we do not even know who to listen to

Especially when we are running away from reality.

Because I was once one of them.

Someone needs to tell about us to ourselves

before it is too late.

To tell about us to anyone else who is listening.

So, I speak for those of us who are not so sure of themselves

as I at this moment. For I am only sure of myself in moments.

So, I take this opportunity, this chance to tell about us to ourselves.

SLOWING DOWN IN TIME!

Train track, clickety clack, time begins to slow.
Oakland at night, Sleeper car.
Crowded, 3:30 am laughter.
A train to explore, a night to adore,
Two girls giggling happily ever after.
Coast Star Lighter!
Slowing down in time!

6:30 am, Oregon morning rhyme.
Breakfast in the dining car
Doors open, slide. Eyes open wide.
Slowing down myself in time. Silence is my prize!

Going back to Corvallis, to a clawfoot tub,
To a bicycle ride at sunset
To an ecstatic moment alive.
Going back in time to Mellon house:
gourmet breakfast; hot tea served to me.
No one else to cook for, just me.
Reading about silence, and living it.

Un struggling, I lay back down in bed after breakfast. I read again and sleep.
Then I do some quilt work, sewing squares together,
taking out the errors, as if someone else had made them.
Sewing, growing ever so appreciative of this moment out of time!
An unheard of peace of mind.
Going back, slowing down in time.
Peddling to town under a clear blue sky to join a hand quilting class,
wind breezing by my face and hair.

Slowing down in time, I find myself again.
This time in row # 57.
I find myself picking blueberries,
in silence after laughter.
I was thirteen again, only happier this time!
I found myself picking blueberries,
Eating blueberries, laughing after blueberries.
Each time I sew the quilt … I find myself and I am overjoyed.

I find silence and I find myself again
Slowing down in time!

LOVE SONG FOR MYSELF

I sing myself a love song: I comfort and cajole.
I cradle the child within. I hold her.
I reach down to enfold her, I tuck her in.

I sing myself this love song. I write my daily score.
I reinvent my body before going out my door.

I am grateful for my teachers; my witnesses; my crew
As I dance along this chosen pathway,
my healing to renew.

I feel my mother's spirit landing on my open palms!

My tears begin to fall when I touch the truth.
I marvel at the psalms.
I reach up to the stars seeking someone else's charms.
I weep in another's arms.
I laugh when our eyes meet.

I sing myself this love song.
I dance! I fly! I play! I remember the tune uncovered
Each step I pray!

I stretch my body and I realign my spine!
Healing laughter lifts me.

On essential food I dine!
Making sense of chaos, finding purpose in all life,
When joyful music fills my soul,
I am limiting my strife!

I see the reflection! I hear the tune!
I swing upon the morning moon!
I grasp the red globe sun. I sit upon the beach.

More than a butterfly, my transformation brings new beginnings.

2009

Age 65

QUAN YIN AND THE DRAGON

I am Quan Yin and The Dragon.
I sent the Unicorn away with other childlike toys.
I have finally awakened and do not wish to play with boys.

The time has come to take my world by storm.
No more time to make excuses. Time for that was overspent!

There is a new day dawning.
and I, The Dragon have been sent!

I Quan Yin, goddess of mercy will lie no more to myself
As I am not satisfied living on a shelf.

I have this tale to tell: Quan Yin and The Dragon leave home at six o'clock.
We leave to go out into the world. We must not stop!

Quan Yin and the Dragon: what a pair!
We will go out and climb the pathway, the golden stair.

I recognize now that my childhood is undone!
Oh, how to tell his tale brings woe.
Now I find I have arrived at a new door and a new sun.

I breathe at last one adult breath and then another.
It has taken me a long time to finally know what I do not know.
I am like my mother.

1978   *Age 34*

ANOTHER FULL MOON RISING

Another full moon rising,
and you are far away.
I know you are safe,
and I know you are well!
I dare not dismay!

Another full moon rising,
like it has many times before.
there's a black and white Daizie dog
Asleep upon the kitchen floor.

She sleeps so calm,
then begins to dream.
Her feet begin to run.
She is chasing you, I imagine
under the bright hot sun.

Up in the sky, above our apple tree,
there's a moon we will always share.
Another full moon rising,
seeing it from here; seeing it from there.

In Boston or at summer camp,
being brave and strong and free,
You build your life now, so independently.
Next year at college in the dorm,
Some day in your own family,
Another full moon you will notice rising
Touching you . . . touching me.

my poetry, my photo journal, my Rap Music, my Rock Opera, my music: my memoir

In my twenties I followed a jazz music group called "Guava" in Berkeley that I went to listen to whenever possible. I was a "groupie". I fell in love with the music and the men who played it.

As I grew older and began to teach in inner city Oakland, I wrote four pieces of Rap music, which I performed to reach students not easy to connect with: "I am Not a 'B' I am not a 'Hoe'"; "Some Teachers Suck and Others are Cool"; "Stayin' Alive"; "In Spanish".

As I aged in Berkeley, I needed to learn how to heal myself. I met a number of alternative healers and learned a lot about how my body was able to heal itself. I choreographed 12 dances and composed the lyrics and wrote a Hero's Journey story to create a Rock Opera called "12 Footfalls" to share with the world what I learned about self-healing.

When I was a teenager, I heard my mother playing piano. She taught herself how to play Chopin on the baby grand piano in our living room. In my youth, I heard my mother singing and playing music from her generation. I sing and listen to 1930's and 1940's music.

In high school I learned to sing all the major Broadway musicals by heart: *Oklahoma, West Side Story, The Pajama Game, The Unsinkable Molly Brown, The Fantastics, Paint Your Wagon.*

As a young independent woman lover in my twenties, I was unbearably lonely. The music I chose to help me through these days and nights was by three torch singers:

Billie Holiday who sang "God Bless the Child Who Has Her Own";

Bessie Smith who sang "Empty Bed Blues" and "My Kitchen Man";

Ida J. Cox who sang "Me, Myself, and I are All In Love With You".

As a teenager I listened to Folkways Records folk music by Pete Seeger, Sonny Terry and Brownie McGee, Muddy Waters, Woody Guthrie and many more traditional folk singers, because my brother Jeff ordered them from Folkways Records and we listened to them. We went to a Pete Seeger concert when I was little and listened to him teaching peace throughout our lives.

My older brother's interest in music influenced me as well. Niki listened to classical music and turned me on to Mozart, and later Franz Schubert's "Trout Quintet" and opera.

When I was a modern dance major student at The Ohio State University, I went to a bar where classical music was played, called "the Library" with my brothers' friends one night and everyone talked about their favorite piece of classical music. I really did not know any. I decided to remember the next piece so I had knowledge of classical music and the next piece was "Pictures at An Exhibition" by Mussorgsky. It remains one of my favorite pieces of music.

My step son Jason listened to Country Western music. One day he came home from a tour in the Gulf War. He was wearing cowboy boots and he brought in a boom box and danced me around the kitchen. So I loved Country Western music.

In San Francisco I heard Earl "Fatha" Heinz, Ella Fitzgerald, Joe Pass, Oscar Peterson, Count Basie, Jean-Pierre Rampal and Keith Jarrett, who played classical/jazz improv extraordinaire.

Rachmaninov's Second Piano Concerto was introduced to me by Larry, when he returned from the Vietnam War where he played clarinet for a year in 1967-1968. He also wrote a piece for us to play called "Adagio Rubato in F for Flute and Clarinet".

I am not a "b" and I am not a "hoe"

Some people think I'm old, cause I am 65,
but I am just startin to jump and jive!

I am not a "b" and I am not a "hoe"
If you don't like me, then you don't know.
I am not an insect and not a roach.
I am not your teacher, I am your COACH.
So I gotta know who my "playahs" are!

I am on your team to help you grow Can I flow?
I don't know.
Teachin is my game, Here is my show:
I know how to help you succeed in time
To mke your life a success . . . Just Rhyme!
If you want to speak Spanish, I am your coach,
But I gotta knbow who my "playahs" are!

Rap

SOME TEACHERS SUCK AND OTHERS ARE COOL! WE ALL WANT YOU TO STAY IN SCHOOL

You came to school to graduate,
Some teachers suck and others are great!
My advice, if choose to hear it:
Find some work you don't hate!
Find a way to cheer it !

Get yourself a job;
Earn a little money;
Get a few friends;
Find yourself a honey!

Find a rhyme.
Stay outta trouble.
Make some time and
Make your money double!
Get a book and pat it!
Take a look at it !

One of my students at Skyline High School

Do not stand on the corner!
Get an education !
Lifelong learning can stop the lamentation!

NO GUNS! NO KILLING! Stay away from the cops!
No dentists! no fillings! Get yourself a job that has props!

Who can Rap ?   ME?
 I want the best for you!
Stay outta trouble if you want a life too.

Get yourself a mouse.   Put it in your house.

NO DRUGS! NO THUGS!
Stay away from the streets in the middle of the night.

Rap

No drive by shootings! No needles! No fight!
Keep your act together
and you'll come out all right!
Remember one lesson from this teacher, old school
Keep your act together!
Survive and be cool!

There is always a choice!
there's a way to survive,
but you have to choose a way to stay alive!
I want you to know, you can make a decision.
Do not accept any kind of derision!

You are the best!
You deserve to rest from the streets, from the crime
that we hear about all of the time.

So, Stay smart!
Drive safe!
Don't drink and drive!
If you are a swimmer, do NOT drink and dive!

SAY NO TO DRUGS!
SAY NO TO THUGS!

If you are addicted, there is a way out!
Twelve step groups do have some clout!

So Get a mouse . . . put it in a house!
Get a job and make a little money!
Know, love, and trust yourself!
Know of all the rest. You truly are the best!
Be in your own bed at night.
Stay outta sight!

Rap

In order to relate on the highest level with my students, I did stand up comedy and wrote Rap songs. I created a Rap to reach out to my students on challenging days. I performed "Stayin' Alive" for the teacher talent show at Skyline High School after 40 years of teaching, with six students sitting on the stage steps pounding out the beat to this rap.

STAYIN' ALIVE

Some teacher somewhere,
may have told you . . . You can't be learnin'
Well, the truth is . . . He or she should be burnin'

Cause everyone of you is fine and fast and smart
All you gotta do . . . is keep your heart open.

Believe in yourself!
That's where it starts!
Get off of that shelf!
Use your own smarts!

Being in high school,
Is a game you are playin'
It's all about knowin'
And all about sayin' what to do
and getting it done.

Two of my students at Skyline High School

Then you can go out and rap in the sun.
Or you can have it
Made in the shade!

Just like your street smarts, you know how to do it!

Join the team before the game starts.

Get to it !

In the street you gotta figure

How to stay alive

The classroom's not different

It's just a new JIVE.

Each teacher has his or her own set of rules

the good ones know You are not fools!

Good teachers want you to face your own fears.

Coaches know you, they know you teach your peers.

At the very first glance

Your coach gives you a chance

once the structure is provided

Let's you make your own rules

Let's you do your own dance.

One of my students at Fremont High summer school

Rap

2003   *Día de Los Muertos, Skyline High School*   *Age 59*

My first rap was written to capture the hearts, hands and minds of my students. To get their attention after dysfunction in the classroom I wrote a rap to connect them. **THEY POUNDED OUT THE "BEAT". I CHANTED THE LINES. THEY SANG THE CHORUS.**

"IN SPANISH"

We are here to learn
Don't get in our way !
Listen up my firiend and you will hear us say:

Chorus:
"We like to rap and we like to dance,
So pay attention and give yourself a chance!
You will learn to speak!
You will learn to sing!
You will learn to think about EVERYTHING

IN SPANISH!   IN SPANISH!   IN SPANISH!"
So, please my fiend
Don't delay!
When you interfere,
you get in your own way!
Build your self esteem!
Go after that dream !
Join the class!
Do it today !

Chorus:
"We like to rap and we like to dance,
So pay attention and give yourself a chance!
You will learn to speak
You will learn to sing
You will learn to think about EVERYTHING

IN SPANISH!   IN SPANISH!   IN SPANISH!"

Rap

I went into peri menopause the same year my daughter began having menstrual periods on Valentine's Day, 2000. We planted a Japanese cherry blossom tree in bloom in front of our home. We created a ritual to support her in this right of passage, this entrance to womanHood.

We found this PMS ZONE greeting card which helped us to have laughter as well as tears at this emotional time.

Moon Lodge Metaphor

17 women came by today to sit in a circle;
to laugh; to play; to celebrate womanhood;
to create a ritual in order to say:
"Love yourself in every way.
Love your body! Love your mind!
Be accepting, whatever you find
inside of you today."

February 14, 2000

"Take time to know just what you need.
Honor yourself! Pay yourself heed!
Many secrets you will discover.
Pay attention to yourself. You will uncover
when you are in flow.
Discover, uncover messages from your center
giving you insight allowing you to enter your mind
allowing you to open your heart."

"Sometimes before we flow, our anger wells up strong
from the pressure on our brain, if we did not sing our song.
Listen to what the voice inside you says, so you will know
Just what the influences are as you grow."

"Never let another person put you down
Let yourself rise in the moon lodge.
Do not go to town."

MOONTIME

"The Moon lodge is a metaphor
To create a place to be nourished
And a place to nurture your body and soul.
Your cycle is a Metaphor too To understand Mother Earth
To see yourself through."

"The moon, the sun, night and day
Summer, Winter, Spring and Fall,
A chance to start over
every month
once and for all.
Every day, month and year
we start over again with a bright little cheer."

The full moon like our bodies waxes and wanes,
As the Ocean's tides are pulled once again,
Our bodies are like the sea as well,
(And Sometimes we feel like we are going to hell.)

NEVER allow anyone to take your self knowledge away from you!

Realize you have a lot of living behind you,
look to notice how it might have refined you.
Your entire life is ahead, do not let it blind you.
Your present is to plan, design and define you.

So, just like the moon as it waxes and wanes
You get to make choices, you get to play games.
You might feel sometimes too many choices it may seem
but you are worthy
to live the life about which you dream.

"Moontime is for renewal, for nourishing our inner strength, for getting in touch with our deepest feelings and for expressing our power. This special time is to reattune to our own personal rhythms we can begin our cycle again pure and strong. It is the time when the Goddess is most likely to use each woman as a channel to pour out her youth and beauty in the form of songs, poems, stories, new ideas and new ideals. Guard this special time of your moon. Don't make yourself so busy that you have no time to do the work of the Goddess, because she brings a blessing for all."

— Flowering Woman *with Shinan Barclay by Mary Dillon*

2015   *Sasha Age 31, Me Age 71*

2014   Sasha Age 30, Me Age 70

womanHood

am I a woman now?
how will I know?
since valentine's day 2000
red blood began to drip down my leg.

I shall never forget this step into
womanHood
three roses from my Dad
and a bag of chocolate gummy bears from my mom later
brought it home to me.

stay home in the moon lodge
to comfort yourself
nurturing yourself
loving yourself
pampering yourself.
Learn to love this new you.
Surround yourself with other woman in their moon time.
Surround yourself with other women creating art.
Remind yourself of this time well spent.

Moan and grown to free your soul,
to howl with the wolves to your heart's content,
to release your discomfort.

You have now joined women throughout all time
though you are probably not sure
that you are willing to do that.
I hold space for you to take your place in womanHood.
I hold you in my heart,
as you cross this threshold,
this right of passage, and I honor you
knowing that the road ahead
is a challenging one!
♥ Mom

Songs I Heard My Mother Sing:

LET ME CALL YOU SWEETHEART

*Let me call you sweetheart. I'm in love with you.
Let me hear you whisper that you love me too.*

*Keep the love light glowing in your eyes so true
Let me call you sweetheart I'm in love with you.*

1981   Faye Silberstein Schwartz   Age 65

LITTLE MAN, YOU'VE HAD A BUSY DAY

*Little man, you're crying, I know why you're blue, Someone took your kitty car away,
Better go to sleep now, Little man, you've had a busy day!*

*Johnny won your marbles, tell you what we'll do, Dad will get you new ones right away,
Better go to sleep now, Little man, you've had a busy day.*

*You've been playin' soldier, the battle has been won The enemy is out of sight,
Come along there soldier, put away your gun, The war is ver for tonight.*

*Time you stop your schemin', time your day was through, Can't you hear the bugle softly say?
Time you should be dreamin' Little man you've had a busy day.*

*Time you should be dreamin'
Rest your weary little head...*

48

SHOO FLY PIE AND APPLE PAN DOWDY

If you want to do right by your appetite
If you're fussy about your food

Take a choo choo today, head New England way
And we'll put you in the happiest mood with

Shoo Fly Pie and Apple Pan Dowdy
Makes your eyes light up

Your tummy says "Howdy"
Shoo Fly Pie and Apple Pan Dowdy

I never get enough of that wonderful stuff
Shoo Fly Pie and Apple Pan Dowdy

Makes the sun come out when Heavens are cloudy
Shoo Fly Pie and Apple Pan Dowdy. I never get enough of that wonderful stuff.

Mama! when you bake Mama! I don't want cake
Mama! For my sake. Go to the oven and make some everlovin'

Shoo Fly Pie and Apple Pan Dowdy
Makes your eyes light up. Your tummy says "Howdy"

Shoo Fly Pie and Apple Pan Dowdy
I never get enough of that wonderful stuff.

Ten Cents A Dance (My Audition Piece):

TEN CENTS A DANCE

I work at the Palace Ballroom, but gee that Palace is cheap;

when I get back to my chilly hallroom I'm much too tired to sleep.

I'm one of those lady teachers, a beautiful hostess, you know

the kind the Palace features for only a dime a throw.

Ten cents a dance, that's what they pay me. Gosh, how they weigh me down!

Ten cents a dance, pansies and rough guys, tough guys who tear my gown!

Seven to midnight I hear drums. Customers crush my toes.

Sometimes I think I've found my hero, but it's a queer romance.

All that you need is a ticket. Come on big boy, ten cents a dance.

Fighters and sailors and bowlegged tailors can pay for their ticket and rent me!

Butchers and barbers and rats from the harbors are sweethearts my good luck has sent me.

Though I've a chorus of elderly beaux, stockings are porous with holes at the toes.

I'm here til closing time. Dance and be merry, it's only a dime.

1963   Lead Dancer in Can-Can at Ohio University   Age 18

It's Only a Paper Moon

Med. Swing

12 FOOTFALLS

"Every footfall is a prayer."

Dancing and self-healing has carried me through my life allowing me to be healthy. I choreographed dances sharing the daily practices of principles by which I live my life to maintain my sanity and to prevent disease. I call this production 12 FOOTFALLS.

SELF-HEALING PRINCIPLE	SET DESIGN	CHOREOGRAPHY
#1 DeStress		Unfolding, unwinding, relaxing, releasing, letting go
		Releasing Inner Critic
#2 Positive Thought		Visualize Healing
		Manifest Positive Thinking
#3 Exercise	Movement Ritual	Dayan Qi Gong
	Tighten & release Muscle Tension	Strengthen and build muscles
		Energy freely flowing clearing blocks
#4 Breathing clean air		Inhale thru nose, exhale thru mouth
		"Inform your body with your breath"
#5 Meditation	Sanskrit Letter "ah" slowing down the brain	Mindfullness / Presence
		Sitting / Standing / Walking
		Stillness & Silence Awakens
#6 Smart Eating	The Body Clock of Healing Energy 	Healing movement during the night
#7 Hydration		Body/mind new cell creation
#8 Community	Silhouette circle	Arrival, embrace, converse
		Avoid isolation
#9 Colon Cleansing	Healthy Cells 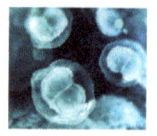	Prevention of cell decay
#10 Spinal realignment	Show spiral spinal rotation	Release tension
	to release tension	Free flow brain muscle message reciprocity
#11 Vertebrae individuation		Slowly sitting up / lying down / sitting up
		to create space between vertebrae
#12 Sleep, restore, renew		"May the moon softly restore you by night"
		Apache Blessing

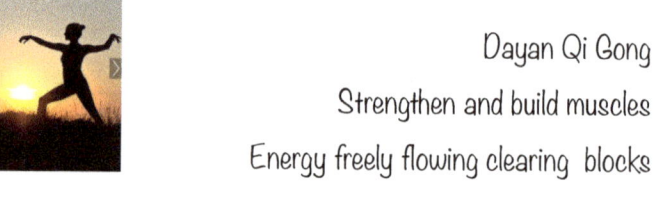

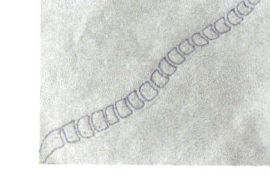

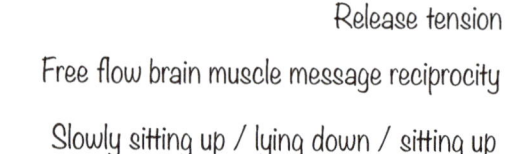

DeStress

Walk in Balance

Release, relax, unwind, let go, allow your body's energy to flow.
Release tension, relax the mind, unwind your body's hold
Take cleansing breaths throughout the day and in the night unfold.

Find harmony, slow down the race.
Walk in balance, find your pace.

Say no to chemical meds. Say no to going to bed for weeks on end.
Say yes to releasing tension and stress.
Say yes to being your own best friend.
Walk daily to realign your spine.
Breathe fresh air in nature in the woods or at the sea.
Say "I love me!"

Find space between your vertebrae.
Find space between thoughts & words & sentences
& paragraphs, ideas & activities.

Do not name the disease. Eradicate it!
Do not kill the cancer cell. Eliminate it!
Let new cells regenerate!
Hold space for self-healing."

dance lyrics #1

Positive Thought

Get Off the Asphalt Road

Harmony is needed, so much comfort is required!
Get off the asphalt roads, they won't us no good!
Get out of the shitty city, get away from the hood!

Hold infinity in the palm of your hand.
Get into the country; get back to the land.

Get out from under the clouds of gray
Move under the sun or get out on the bay.
Get off the asphalt road! It ain't going any where!
Get under a waterfall and wash your hair!

On your Hero's journey
You may find some asphalt roads. Do not go there!
Instead search for your wisdom! Find your prize!
Align your spirit and get back home to the other side!
Sail on you dreamer, get out to sea!
Look up and follow the stars to infinity.

Positive thought practice.
I am loved and I deserve love.
I will be who I am and I am enough.
I trust myself and I can trust others.
I respect myself and I deserve respect from others.

dance lyrics #2

Qi Gong

Music Is My Religion

Music is my religion. It saves me every day!
All I need is music to send me on my way.
When I sing, when I play, I live my heart's way!

You can live in the desert, on the prairie, or
On the ocean sand.
You can play the guitar, flute or drums.
You can bring your own little band.

I sing songs that carry me.
I channel music down from heaven.
Music is my religion. This is the prayer that calls my name.
Music is my religion. I have god in all her glory.
Music is in my soul. Thru music I tell my story.

God channel music down from heaven,
Or bring it up from hell.
It doesn't matter from where it comes.
It will make me well !

The whole world can hear it when I play.
Just like god can hear it, when I pray.
Keep the music coming. Then one fine day,
the world will be healed, that's what I pray.

We must practice
to be wise, to be healed, to be free.
Music is my religion. My song will heal me.
I play my music every day.
I self heal disease away.

dance lyrics #3

Breathing Clean Air

Inform Your Body With Your Breath

Say yes to breathing clean air.
Our body, our organs, our muscles are informed by breathing clean air.
We have more energy; we have more liberty.
Oxygen brings health to muscles: keeping them from cramping.

Breathing clean air is required.
Every day, every night in the morning and in the evening.
Taking breaks throughout the day is a key to restoring our health.
Reminding ourselves to breath consciously
helps to remove or to take tension away.
It helps our organs to recover from stress.
Take cleansing breaths as a gift every day;
3 to 5 breaths as a gift that is what they say.
Inhale thru the nose; exhale thru the mouth, several times each day.

Find release and harmony.
Find peace in a life that used to be stressful!
Inform your body with your breath.

dance lyrics #4

Meditation

I Can Not Work For Money

I just can not work for money any more!
It doesn't do the trick!
I can not search for meaning that way
it will only make me sick.
I know I must be nourished and nurtured by my work
Rock my soul with my job or be a soda jerk!
Do not waste my life dangling a carrot before my eyes
Do not rob me any more, it is time I realize.
I need work that fills me up, fills my needs, fills my cup.
I want to find my heart full at the end of EVERY day
I must find myself a job that will harmonize within me
and I am willing to pay!
I need to find me some work, I need to be fulfilled
I want to engage in promising existence so every day I am thrilled.
I will get me a job! I will get me a life! and I will become highly skilled!
and we already know that everybody needs a wife!

Use the eyes to slow down the brain
Following the Sanskrit letter "ah".
Chant to bring the mind to stillness.
Live in silence.
Free the mind.

dance lyrics #5

Smart Eating

The Human Body Energy Clock

Knowing when you are hungry will fend off sickness sure!
Do not eat unless you require food as sustenance.
That is one cure.
Know if you are truly hungry, before you take another bite.
If your body is your temple, treat it right!
Do not use food as medication in the day or in the night!

Staying healthy is a full time job.
Getting well is a practice too.
Know about your body clock.
It can bring a saving grace to you.

Do not ever eat past seven, so your body clock can thrive.
Metabolism takes all night you know.
To keep your body alive.
Time is required for your organs to metabolize food that is smart to eat.

Do not try to fill the holes in your psyche with food.
You must not fool yourself this way any longer.
You need to be filled with a vibrant life force.
Calm your cravings.
You are getting stronger.

Satisfy your emotions! Do not feed them!
Stop feeding your addictions.
Support your mind with positive thought.

Eat well! Eat right! Eat smart!
Exercise to metabolize! Save your heart!
Hike, ride, swim or practice Qi Gong
to keep your energy flowing.

Ask yourself: Am I hungry? Am I happy?
Do not eat to quell the pain.
Find a way to eat for sustenance
that is one solution to gain.

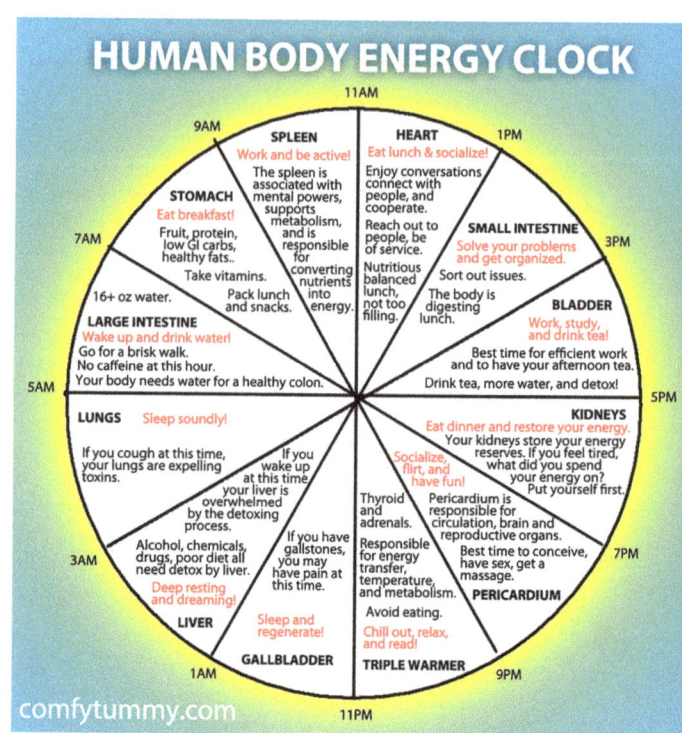

dance lyrics #6

Hydration

Hydration Chant

The human body depends on water to survive.
Every cell, tissue, organ needs water to thrive. Hydrate.

Water is needed
for the body: to maintain temperature; to remove waste; to lubricate joints;
for overall good health.

Facts about water:
> brain is 80% H_2O
> blood contains 83% H_2O
> lungs contain 79 % H_2O
> muscles contain 76% H_2O

Every function of the body is dependent on a steady supply and flow of water.

Water transports hormones, chemicals and nutrients which are vital to efficient organ function.

Without water we would not be able to digest or absorb minerals or nutrients and our kidneys would fail from toxic overload.

Water is a miracle elixir:
> Water keeps skin vibrant and supple;
> Escorts toxins from the body;
> Supports healthy metabolism;
> Improves energy;
> Removes body heat;
> Lubricates joints;
> Improves mental and physical performance;
> Supports digestion.

Water Not only sustains life but holds within it the capacity to heal.

Remember: By the time you are thirsty, your body is already dehydrated.

dance lyrics #7

Community

dear god, dear goddess

dear god, dear goddess, dear mother earth
hear us now.
dear trees, dear spirit, dear ocean, dear dolphins near us,
dear whales far away.
I forgive myself ! I forgive you!
we begin again in love.
we have gone astray!

most of your children are living in pain.
we watch each other dying in fear!
we are going insane.

raise up to sing to the world around us,
sing about hope! sing about dope!
sing about everything that matters,
before our whole earth shatters!
sing to us about positive thought
and evolution, too.

teach your children what to say
and they will teach us what to do.
bring your children home to you.

dear god, dear goddess, dear mother earth
hear us now
we pray and meditate by dancing
self care is our mantra

we sit down and stand up in community.

dance lyrics #8

Colon Cleansing

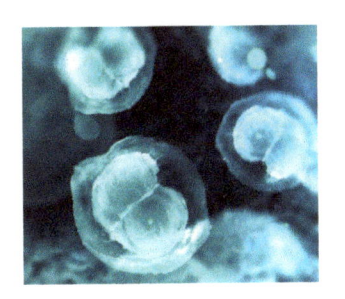

What Is The Toll?

Do not stay young.　　　　　　Do not grow old.
Rock your body!　　　　　　　Rock your soul!
Rock personal wisdom!　　　　Recovery Roll!
　　　　　That is the toll.

Listen to wise harmonies.
Allow your body to rise and shine!
Allow your life source to fly! Stay on top of your own creation.
Don't let too much time go by.
Save your whole world by creating intervention.
Follow your intention.

Stay on top of who you are !
Rock your body. Rock your soul! Keep em going strong.
Rock your intestines! Keep em clean all day and all night long.
Keep your colon clean. No cells will decay. No cancer will develop.
The body finds its balance.
Clean colon enables you to live life long.
Clear, clean intestines, healthy cells is the answer to this song:
Shake it out tomorrow! It will heal you all night long.

Don't dare use chemotherapy. *(Dr. Gerson, 1930)*

Rock your body! Rock your soul!
Cleanse your emotions, mind, and colon.
That is the toll!
Save your body. Save your soul.

100% of your energy
is available each day for self-healing instead of digestion.

dance lyrics #9

Spinal Realignment

Life Brings Us Freedom

Life brings us freedom. Life brings us pain.
We have many paths to guide us.
We have something to gain.
We can NOT face distraction.
Focus is the key.
Our focus must guide us to our destiny.
Or to oblivion we flee.

We seek our guides when we are lost.
Forbidden pathways lie unknown.
Focus is required, just like the stars on high.
We need to learn to trust ourselves.

We must know where we are headed,
Or lost we'll always be.
We need to trust our tour guides to show us
how focus can bring us liberty.
No longer can we pardon our careless youthful ways.
Distraction can divide us.
We must find one another and make every day our day of days.

Life brings us freedom on the hero's journey home.

The stars remain a constant. The stars, the sky and the sea!
I picked the stars to guide me
when I was a kid in search of Me.

Guide us now. Show us how
to bring ourselves home once more.
Bring ourselves to freedom now we are ready to know the real score.

When we find one pathway ends
We can notice a brand new door.

dance lyrics #10

Vertebrae Individuation

A Hero's Journey

A hero's journey takes us all.
On path unknown we ride from the land of origin
far away to another side.
We travel the road
as adventure calls us.
We dare not answer "no".
It enthralls us to decide to go.

From our ordinary world
those who answer the calls are few.
Some refuse. They say "No! No!"
Adventureff? Some of us can not resist.

We meet our mentors one by one
Wisdom, guide, and Shakti,
Commit ourselves to the task we must,
or fall to the side and refuse.

We get to lose our ego.
We discover sites anew.
After initiation we know it's time to return.
We meet back with our crew.

dance lyrics #11

"May The Moon Softly Restore You By Night"

A Hero's Journey Home

On our hero's journey home, we are tested repeatedly.
We discover enemies, whom we did not know.
We find side kicks, even allies as we approach our inmost cave.
We must decide who's safe to know; who brings trouble to us;
who to leave behind and whom it is we want to save.

Seek we our own elixir, not knowing the design.
We follow the road back home to our community,
not remembering where it is.
Confronting the dark side to find the light
not knowing who we are going to be.

Face we the last ordeal.
We find a choice of death or survival.
Then resurrection calls us and we return back archival
to the "ordinary world".

Back to the community from which we have come,
We carry our elixir in our hand
To show our friends the gift.
By some we are welcomed to the land.

The story is an old one lived by many women and men.
This hero's journey is a long one.
It takes us so far away and leads us home again.

We travel far and wide to seek wisdom, mentors one and all.
If we come upon a crisis of faith we may think it is a sin.
We learn to climb out again!

As many heroes do on their hero's journey home,
presenting our elixir. We are welcomed back to our land.

We may forget about the trauma. We may forget about the pain.
We must learn to accept ourselves our fate, our new elixir and our new name.

dance lyrics #12

Healers' Wisdom heard by Sondra Schwartz

"The body has the ability to heal itself."
— 1930 Dr. Gerson

" Begin your day eating only one fruit until you eliminate." [for back pain]
— 1972 Mildred Jackson: "Alternatives to Chemical Medicine"

"For every tear you cry you live an hour longer."
— 1973 Marion Rosen: Gentle Rocking massage therapist

"Keep your colon clean and your body will heal itself."
— 1974 Hal Stewart: Health Store on 38th St. / Mac Arthur Avenue

"Juicing allows the body to use its energy to heal the body rather than to spend its energy in digestion."
— 1974 Dr. Paavo Airola

Follow the Sanskrit letter "ah" to slow down the brain.
Chant to find stillness and silence.
— 1972 Rimpoche Tartant Tulku, Tibetan Nyingma Institute

"All my relations." — spoken by shaman entering the sweat lodge
"The rocks are your teachers. Face your fear. Name it. Walk beyond it."
The native Americans were curing AIDS with the Sun Dance."
— Lakota Sioux Native American Robert Greywing in a sweat lodge.
Native Americans use natural herbs for healing.

"When injured, stop doing everything until you heal completely.
Reduce the Stress. Learn to manage the pain, rebuild the muscles."
— 1978 Dr. Martin Shaffer: "Life After Stress"

"Inform your body with your breath. Realign your spine and individuate your vertebrae.
Release the Psoas muscle to eliminate back pain."
— 1999 Anna Halprin

Natural Medicine Cabinet For the 21st Century

Ginger tea dissolves kidney stones, cleanses liver, reduces joint pain.

Raw honey kills every kind of bacteria scientist can throw at it.
It cures and combats diseases.

Cinnamon lowers blood sugars.

Tumerick combats inflammation; good for many other benefits.

Jerusalem Artichokes: eaten fresh (synthetic cortisone) heals joint pain.

White willow bark has natural salicylic acid.

Golden seal: natural antibiotic prevention of
colds, allergies, urinary tract infections, cancer.
It boosts the immune system.

Echinacea helps boost the immune system.

DL Lysine is an amino acid used in biosynthesis of proteins.
Prevents colds related to herpes.

Rescue remedy: place under the tongue when trauma occurs.

Barley is better for digestion than rice.

Mung beans prevent constipation and assist in digestive efforts.

Adzuki beans prevent and manage diabetes.
Also assists in digestion.

Wu Mei (**dried plums**) decrease inflammation and arthritis pain.

Lecithin improves heart health and lowers cholesterol.

Nutritional yeast: known as brewer's yeast.
High in vitamin B
Raises level of good cholesterol

Vitamins
Vitamin D can help prevent vertigo.

Vitamin C helps heal colds and flu.

Calcium Magnesium.

"*Garlic* is as good as ten mothers."
A Natural antibiotic

Astragalus root: boosts the immune system

Goji Berries: reduces inflamation

Black sesame seeds: healthy heart, skin/bones, anti-aging and good for digestive health

Apple Cider Vinegar: foot fungus, skin disruption, diluted to resolve minor colds and bacterial infection.

Cucumber: lowers blood presdure naturally

Qi Gong: gentle Chinese martial arts exercise to help keep energy flowing for self-healing.

Epsom Salts for bathing.

Insomnia resolutions:
Massage insomnia point at the front of the heel.
Walk barefoot on the grass 5 minutes.

*My father told me when he was 65
that the hardest thing about being this age
is when friends your own age are dying.*

1926   Mike Schwartz Head Shot   Age 17

After my long time friend, lover, jazz pianist improvisor died last April
I found this poem that helped me to grieve.

No Coming and No Going
— thich nhat hanh

This body is not me.
I am not limited by this body.
I am life without boundaries.
I have never been born,
and I have never died.

Look at the ocean and the sky filled with stars,
manifestations from my wondrous true mind.

Since before time, I have been free.
Birth and death are only doors
through which we pass,
sacred thresholds on our journey.
Birth and death are a game of hide and seek.

So laugh with me,
Hold my hand,
Let us say good-bye,
Say good-bye, to meet again soon.

We meet today.
We will meet again tomorrow.
We will meet at the source every moment.
We meet each other in all forms of life.

About the Author

My parents met in the theater. They were actors.
They were social workers.
They taught me to fight for freedom and justice.
They modeled love, understanding, compassion and democracy.
They once had a love for the ages,
until the doctors destroyed it.

At age 74, I am so very sensitive, I cry at the drop of a hat, at weddings or when hearing Auld Lang Syne sung every New Year's Eve, for all the years lost and my nostalgia for wasting them.

I am deeply touched often to tears, poignantly with music, theater and during the sermon at the Unitarian Universalist Congregation of Marin where a young minister, whom I knew growing up with my daughter, tells stories and weaves hope from our current fearful political world.

Tears come to the surface in my heart mind and eyes nearly every day in nostalgia, in grief and in poignancy.

I have met a few "talk" therapists, with whom I had a good fit. I was able to resolve a few issues growing up, but did not complete my adolescence until my late twenties or thirties.

As a clean and sober adult, I am the only one I know, who does not take chemical medicine to alleviate depression. I did have a challenging period in the sixties and seventies where I used alcohol and drugs, which I thoroughly enjoyed, but for which I paid a high price emotionally. I arrived in San Francisco in 1968 during the "summer of love". I wore " flowers in my hair" and bell bottom trousers. I was a hippie, although I did not call myself one. I was vibrantly alive during the "free love" era, so I explored and enjoyed sex throughout my 20's and 30's.

(I wrote and published a book *A Woman Awakening: Orgasmic Evolution of a A Time Traveler*.)

One most gentle lover I enjoyed, from whom I learned Tantra, was a Jazz Pianist who had "the best foreplay I ever heard." Because I was desperate and alone, I hooked up with him when I was 28 and began using drugs and was playing in a dangerous physical and psychological world.

I became addicted to marijuana, hash oil and cocaine in my thirties. I have been clean and sober for thirty three years. (Jim died from alcohol and drug abuse last April. I mourn his loss.) I worked a recovery program called ACA (Adult Children of Alcoholics), and Alanon (for family members of Alcoholics). For the last two years I have been working in a 12 step program called CoDA (Codependents Anonymous) where I learned how to set boundaries and take care of myself rather than trying to take care of others.

Choreographing Twelve Footfalls

I choreographed this rock opera and wrote the lyrics and music when seeking purpose in my life, after my divorce and break up of my family 12 years ago.

My Mom had been erroneously diagnosed with cancer and put in a mental institution when I was six. I never lost the trauma and devastation that developed from my feelings of abandonment. (I have that in common with other members of CoDA .)

I grew up not trusting western medicine nor western medical doctors because my Mom taught me not to trust them after her mother's ten back surgeries and her own bad treatment by the "quack", who misdiagnosed her with uterine cancer, and treated her for two years and then disappeared, nor the psychiatrist who put her in Harding's Sanatarium and gave her shock therapy.

(I had one trusted western doctor, my childhood doctor, Dr. Frye, who made house calls.)

I was determined not to be diagnosed or misdiagnosed with cancer. My Mom taught me not to trust the western medical community (or anyone I dare say.)

1952   *Mom Age 36, Dad Age 43*

    When my parents were young, before my Mom was misdiagnosed with uterine cancer, they spent time at Art Galleries and our family played ball together on the OSU campus. Everyone thought our family was the Ozzie and Harriet perfect family until the trouble began.

I ran away from home to Berkeley, California and I set out, in my life, as I needed help, to heal myself from my childhood trauma and from my adult illnesses, to learn self-healing from the alternative medical community.

I was introduced to juicing by Dr. Paavo Airola in a book called *How To Get Well*.

I learned that the human body was capable of self-healing potential and prevention of illness.

Seeking purpose after divorce and retirement, I decided to share with the world the 12 principles that I practice to prevent and cure disease.

I choreographed 12 dances to model practices of these 12 principles, by which I have lived, in order to use my body's ability to heal itself. I spent my life searching for and finding natural healers, to introduce safe natural healing techniques and natural herbal medicines, so that I could live a sane and healthy life.

I wrote the story of the Hero's Journey Home and the lyrics to songs from all types of music, in order to introduce the body's ability to achieve self-healing to people who enjoyed all genres of music. "Twelve Footfalls" is the rock opera that tells the story of me, the hero going out into an unknown world and finding the "elixir" to heal the world (Tikun Olam), which is the practices of principles that allow the body to heal itself.

My Mom lived in New York City in the Theater District on West 48th St. right off Broadway. She wrote 28 plays. She made all of her own clothes, sewing by hand for the last 20 years of her life. She walked a mile and back to the library and to the grocery store in her seventies, when she lived in the Fruitvale District of Oakland. One time when she came to San Francisco she chose to live in the Tenderloin District because she could afford it. It was walking distance from the Theater District. She was a tough lady.

One year she lived near downtown Oakland, when I was running the Sailboat house at Lake Merritt. She could walk over to the lake and walk around it, which she sometimes did when I was on the rescue power boat on the lake.

When my daughter was one year old in 1985, my Mom lived in Oakland, in the Fruitvale District before it became Hispanic. I walked with Sasha in the stroller for a mile and back to visit her on Shabbat Friday evenings. She made my daughter a jump rope out of material that she bought for ten yards for a dollar in 1986. She lived on $238 from Social Security. She never believed in charge accounts. She paid for everything in cash including her 1965 Slant Six Plymouth Valiant Convertible for $2200. (Which I learned how to tune up myself, and even how to change the shoe brakes.)

My Dad spoke Yiddish, played the violin and told jokes in Yiddish to the Golden Agers. He directed theater shows at the Columbus Jewish Community Center in the 1950's and 1960's. He was a man for all seasons, every body liked him or so it seemed. Our house in Columbus was walking distance to the JCC, which meant that I could walk over to see him after my parents got divorced, one of the hardest times in my life.

My Mom worked in a Settlement House in Pittsburgh, Pennsylvania when they met.

My Mom earned a Bachelor's Degree from OSU. My Dad earned a Master's Degree in Social Work at OSU.

Buddhist mantra dedication to peace in the world and in my heart, my mind and my life —

May I be safe.

May I live at ease.

May I be calm.

May I live in peace and harmony.

May I live in equanimity.

May I walk in balance.

May the world be safe.

May the world live at ease.

May the world be calm.

May the world live in peace and harmony.

May the world live in equanimity.

May we all walk in balance!

1972   *San Miguel de Allende Artista*   *Age 89*

"We are all going to die. None of us know when.
What is important is to live and to love and to laugh."
— IRA GAFFIN
*Spoken to me when high school friend
had full blown Aids in 1994 due to transfusions.*

"TEACH from ECSTATIC MOMENT to ECSTATIC MOMENT."
Successful teaching is made this way.
— DR. RICHARD MOSIER
*Professor Philosophy of Education
Heidegger "Being and Time"
UC Berkeley graduate seminar*

"Tomorrow is another day !"
"Lie down and rest when you are tired."
— FAYE FRANCIS SILBERSTEIN (MY MOM)

"One day at a time!"
"If your ass falls off, put it in bag
and take it to a meeting!"
"Don't take yourself so seriously.
You are not the center of the universe."
— BOB HOOD

CPSIA information can be obtained
at www.ICGtesting.com
Printed in the USA
BVHW020448250519
548866BV00005B/51/P